GeNtry!fication: *or* the scene of the crime

By Chaun Webster

Book Cover Design: Douglas Kearney
Book Interior Design: Chaun Webster and Sarah Gzemski
Cover image sourced from the John R. Borchert Map Library at the
University of Minnesota.

Published by Noemi Press, Inc. A Nonprofit Literary Organization.
www.noemipress.org.

*This book was made possible in part through a private donation in memory of
Namba and Yvonne Roy.*

GeNtry!fication: *or* the scene of the crime

By Chaun Webster

Contents

Prologue
Acknowledgements
Ntro
black bodies *or* the scene of the crime
north minneapolis circa 1492
U.S. Urbanity: a folktale
Do. Not. Enter.
Quantum FEET

***

Communiqué de Whoopin': *or* the child runs faster than *trouble*
legibility *or* the scene of the crime
"i don't want no fucking country"
black bodies en fugue
Theft *or* the scene of the crime

***

Communiqué #1
nah...
maybe   home
natural areas: middle segment 1935 *or* some maps have an afterlife
because apparently no one woke up on they john wayne shit to
take land. it just happened...
this is not a black   *Atlantic*
this is not a black   out
gentry.

***

Communiqué #2
huh?
this is not a ~~black~~. and it is.
talking commodities *or* the scene of the crime
N's in molecular type
forbidDIN

Communiqué #3
this is not a black: an abstraction on a nonessential thing
GeNtry!fication: a 21st century disappearing act
i remember
bodies out of place

***

Communiqué #4
darkMATTER *or* detour
blackness is a constant act of flight

***

Communiqué #5
rən
foot notes

***

Communiqué #6
a murder of crows *or* the scene of the crime
this is not a black: a note on instability.

***

Communiqué #7
i don't remember
DARK**matter** *or* retour

***

Communiqué #8
run.
Astro Colony *or* an Obscure Rock in the Milkyway will Gentrify
also: the scene of the crime
yup...

gawn!
Notes
Bibliography / Nods / Samples And Suggested Tea

Prologue

Acknowlededements

Thank you to Douglas Kearney for reviewing these poems in there earliest stages and the generosity of your feedback, your work taught me how to reckon with din as a kind of black study. So grateful for all you do.

To the editors at, *Public Pool*, for publishing versions of these poems, my gratitude.

To Diana Arterian, Suzi Garcia, Carmen Giménez Smith, and Sarah Gzemski, for reading and believing in this work and challenging it to be better. Noemi is the illest and I am so honored to have this work find a home there.

Aaron Mallory, Jimmy Patiño, Jose Luis Villasenor, Jermaine Ross Allum, Filiberto Nolasco Gomez, Vichet Chhuon, ya'll are squad. Thanks for talking shit with me.

Foremost, to Verna Wong, for helping me carve out space, and supporting me through every iteration. Love you immensely.

And to all those doing the hard work of naming the crime precisely and tearing this whole bidness down, thank you for seeing beyond the rubble too. One.

perhaps we are maroons, tricksters tucking the north star beneath our tongues. maybe we will not forget this time the theft wrapped in the sheepskin of our own vernacular, the land grabs, nooses made of rope or service weapon. maybe this time we've learned the lessons of too many robberies, learned to speak our names in secret.

Ntro

Lorde taught you. Baraka too. About being out. "Animal stories, the descendant of the answer."[1] Dig? "That dream was never mine."[2] We out, like, way, way out. Like "outside of value."[3] So who the fuck you trying to convince? And we believe in blackness.[4] Study dat'. Believe dat'. Lovin' that interior more than the haunted house of "Negro Slum", fabricated presence, the prison that visibility built. Nah, we gawn! Check the receipts. Foot notes. This ain't never been for us. Development or re-development. Both sounding like our disposability. Both depending on them stories Baldwin talked about, them stories "designed to reassure us that no crime was committed." And sometimes black hands wielding Thor's hammer too. And I smell robbery everywhere. Nah. We with Kameelah, "refusing to be legible."[5] Ran. Away. And strung together from them notices I read a folktale. Of refusal. Can you see it? Between the lines. Beneath the attempt to make the subject, inventory. All our children racing trouble. And what that M. NourbeSe Phillip say? "The smallest cell remembers."[6] Remember? Like them feet crossing mason dixie. To the up south. You know the story? Of them feet that outran the twister?

Ran down Freeeemont Avenue. Twister spinning all kinda' disaster capitalism. That child ran barefoot not knowing the outcome, but willing theyself elsewhere, willing a future and a geography unable to swallow them whole. Catch me there, *speaking our names in secret*.

Chaun Webster
North Minneapolis, MN
October 2017

1. See Amiri Baraka, *Tales Of The Out & The Gone,*160.

2. See the notes section under, *gawn!*, and give thanks. The Lorde is good.

3. See Lindon Barret, *Blackness and Value: Seeing Double.*

4. See Ashon Crawley's elaboration of Moten's concept of Black Study, *Blackpentecostal Breath: The Aesthetics of Possibility*, 3.

5. See the notes section under, *darkMATTER or detour*, for more on Kameelah Rasheed.

6. See M. NourbeSe Phillip, *She Tries Her Tongue, Her Silence Softly Breaks*, 37.

Black bodies *or* the scene of crime

stage
as in, the popular theater
of your body.
on a corner
at a benchless bus shelter -
sittin' yo ass on that pavement.

stage
you not supposed to be here
yet you are -
some natural contradiction.
your snarl and ravenous appetite—
fiction. an imagined geography.

stage
a secondhand body
not even your own.
a market of amusement.

stage
marching onto the 19
late again
to take you elsewhere.

north minneapolis north minneapolis north minneapolis
north minneapolis north minneapolis north minneapolis
north minneapolis north minneapolis north minneapolis
north minneapolis north minneapolis north minneapolis
north minneapolis north minneapolis north minneapolis
north minneapolis north minneapolis north minneapolis
north minneapolis north minneapolis north minneapolis
north minneapolis north minneapolis north minneapolis
north minneapolis north minneapolis north minneapolis
north minneapolis north minneapolis north minneapolis
north minneapolis north minneapolis north minneapolis
north minneapolis north minneapolis north minneapolis
north minneapolis north minneapolis north minneapolis
north minneapolis north minneapolis north minneapolis
north minneapolis north minneapolis north minneapolis
north minneapolis north minneapolis north minneapolis
north minneapolis north minneapolis north minneapolis
north minneapolis north minneapolis north minneapolis
north minneapolis north minneapolis north minneapolis
north minneapolis north minneapolis north minneapolis
north minneapolis north minneapolis north minneapolis
north minneapolis north minneapolis north minneapolis
north minneapolis north minneapolis north minneapolis
north minneapolis north minneapolis north minneapolis
north minneapolis north minneapolis north minneapolis
north minneapolis north minneapolis north minneapolis
north minneapolis north minneapolis north minneapolis
north minneapolis north minneapolis north minneapolis
north minneapolis north minneapolis north minneapolis
north minneapolis north minneapolis north minneapolis
north minneapolis north minneapolis north minneapolis
looks a lot like the scene of a robbery circa 1492.

U.S. Urbanity: a folktale

our concentration   marked us   vile
so we elected ourselves   bandits

jackals howling
cunning things
by morning

the whole earth
bled overnight

but we lick dry bones   too

and there is *witness*
wedged between our
teeth

each solitary
stretch of the diaspora
says, "runaway child."

Communiqué de Whoopin':
or the child runs faster than *trouble*

so the child. yeah, the child. they be a ____
fast runner

      got Assata feet.
      got Tubman in they soles.
      run like Usain, they do.

fast enough to maroon, to move between here(s).
                                     that child here.
- beautiful production of **black** spirit and fleshhh - hear - wanna
race *trouble*.

wanna stride cleeeeeeeeeeeaaaaarrrr cross the diaspora.

wanna mooooooooovvve atop the water like some say
the son of man did long time ago,
'cept they not walking.

this child fix it in they mind that they 'gon race. that. *trouble*.
'gon meet up with it on some corner
(we'll say the corner of Lowry and Penn) good kin in company.

      corner full of liquor and contained absence.
      corner bearing name of St. Cloud slave master
      corner curating sex work & evacuated names.

gon meet up there - there - there -there

legibility *or* the scene of the crime

a ~~geography~~ that is badly designed will be illegible.

10 point Baskerville

a geography ~~that~~ is ~~badly~~ designed ~~will be illegible~~.

10 point Futura

a geography ~~that~~ is b~~adly~~ ~~designed~~ ~~will be~~ illegible.

10 point Adobe Garamond Pro

"i don't want no fucking country"

for Dionne Brand

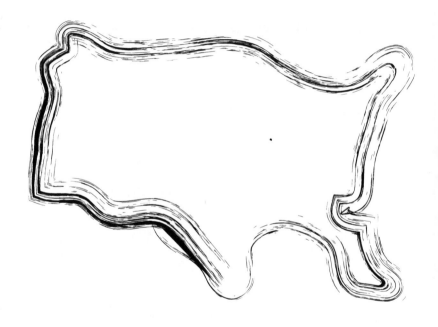

black bodies en fugue

" redevelopment schemes have recurrently precipitated widespread
displacement of the lowest-capital

residents living in sites deemed concentrations of poverty. And they
must. residents

and places serve the ground for visions of redevelopment.

Theft *or* the scene of the crime

something was stole
but it wasn't that 20 dollars
from the register.
yeah, something was robbed.
it will not register -
incalculable
but underneath the skin.
the scene of some crime.

mutha fucka you don't belong here

something ain't right.
outta place - behind the register.
you look there
behind   *there*.
below some bosses' accusation
preceded by a thousand others
but you the only one (**t**)here *mutha fucka*

YOU   don't belong

then, something happens -
is happening, always.
on the tip of your tongue.
like a gun
pulled for a heist.
go on child —
HOWL!!

Communiqué #1

maybe home

maybe black is not a home nor a country as Baraka called it nor any essential thing. maybe black is but the imperfect signifier we carry on our way. maybe black is not a home nor a country as Baraka called it nor any essential thing. maybe black is but the imperfect signifier we carry on our way. maybe black is not a home nor a country as Baraka called it nor any essential thing. maybe black is but the imperfect signifier we carry on our way. maybe black is not a home nor a country as Baraka called it nor any essential thing. maybe black is but the imperfect signifier we carry on our way. maybe black is not a home nor a country as Baraka called it nor any essential thing. maybe black is but the imperfect signifier we carry on our way.

NATURAL AREAS
MIDDLE SEGMENT
MINNEAPOLIS · 1935

because apparently no one woke up on they john wayne shit to take land. it just happened...

apparently no one rose
mouth full of robbery -
apparently no one intends to take the land

now when i say land i mean body

and no one designed the erasure.
no one landed on the disappeared.
no one spoke the topography
of three bodies swallowed by fire -
no more   no   more no more.
no one poofed the land

i mean the body

from the earth / another body holding our own.

this land

and by land i mean this body

is not our own. and no one done that.

this is not a black *Atlantic*

this is not a black. this is a lap around a country without coordinates. this is what lay between and around the subject. hocus pocus and other disappearances, runnings away. this is not a black. this is the black that wasn't that the black that was hid within. this is the black vote that isn't, the invoked poor and working class cannon fodder. this is fabricated presence. this is not a black, and get that black name that wasn't — out your mouth, that is. this is not a black, this is a series of names for non-black things that were black or not. a practice in madness. this is a city of bones. a re presented thing. this is not a black. this is not a black. this is not a black. this is not. this is not. black. this is. not black. this is not. this is not a. black this is not. this is. this is. not black. this is. not black. this is not a. this is not a. a. black

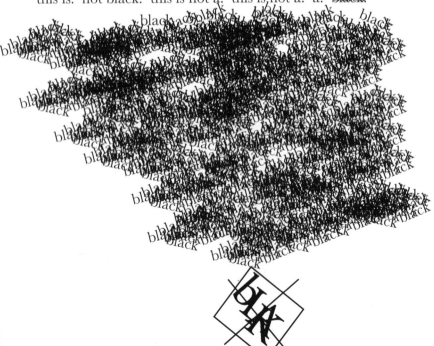

gentry.

Communiqué #2

cutting this way and that way with they feet.
the kind of dance that conjures -

yeah furious thing it was - and fore you know it child was
rolling up that scroll nice and tight. tying hemp around it and
throwing it over they back as they make they way to
the corner.

child makin' they way to that corner to see if *trouble* come to resolve
the terms of they whoopin'.

but *trouble* don't show.

too busy doin' what *trouble* always done...makin' trouble.

maybe this time in some Houston cell.
or maybe at a doorstep in some sundown town.

or maybe along Plymouth Avenue N after a party.

or maybe - - or maybe - or maybe

or maybe

trouble be in many places at once with they 'bidness.

so child don't pay no mind to waiting

huh ?

this is not a ~~brick.~~

talking commodities *or* scene of the crime

i know a commodity that spoke.
a once-valued thing,
speaking -

mumbling something
on the corner of Lowry and Penn,
up from the dusk of some northside mythology.
i know of surplus
of waste
of what was left
and is now leaving -
fugitive.

i know maroon
and too much liquor
neighboring
our "too-soon
babies."

i know a man face
bloodied walking bottle
in hand midday down
the block, blight
surrounding him

40 oz caressing his exaggerated face
who when

asked "are you alright?"
screams, wails.
and riding underneath
that prolonged noise that cuts between the *witness*
in his teeth, i hear:

"ARE ANY OF US!!??"

N in molecular type

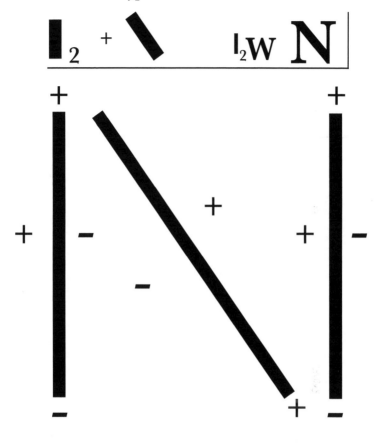

N is formed by two binaries that have overlapped and bonded with the W imagination. These binaries are the framework for designating undersirable bodies and speculating on desirable land. Same charge repulsion between each face of the W imagination and its respective facing binary face cause the N to hold its shape.

forbid**DIN**

din | din

noun [in sing.]
a loud, unpleasant, and prolonged voice: *the negroes
made a forbidDIN and awful noise!! "din is discourse"*

Communiqué #3

the child don't pay no mind to waiting

rather
        sends two **black birds** in the sky

with the   **Communiqué De Whoopin'**

the stately appeal to the niggas on they block.

then sprinkles some Mississippi on they feet and

MOOOOOOOOOOOOOOOVVVVVVVESSS they way along

Freemont, Emerson, West Broadway, Vincent, Girard

speaking what sound like the good news. like the gospels according to

    LORDE
    DAVIS
    SMITH
    & WELLS-BARNETT

now you may be asking yourself, if *trouble* known to be making so much trouble why don't they just show up to hear some silly terms? some outrageous challenge from a child?

and it'd be due to the coward that *trouble* be.

this is not a black: an abstraction on a nonessential thing

this is not a

GeNtry! fiction: a 21st century disappearing act

negroes, surrounded.
surrounding:
a business district
industrial
a gold coast.

like a stain
a sea, venereal disease.
negroes somewhere
in your pants.
somewhere down under,
not fucking-
fucked.

negroes.
fucking   negroes
land full of borders
illegible inhabitants of the uninhabitable.
negroes, legible when danger.
negroes, a fairy tale-
a magic trick.
negroes, now you see them...

negroes negroes negroes negroes negroes negroes negroes negroes
negroes negroes negroes negroes

SHAZAM!!

...now you don't.

i remember...

~~bodies~~ out of place

a ~~body~~ was "out of place."
you know the story, its arch and its end:

the artificial borders drawn in *The Book of Negroes* -
or a runaway notice
or the description of a just-barely-beatable enemy
by a county attorney.

narratives, consonant over time.

you know this story. it doesn't surprise you:

someone "reached for   "
"had a   "
"resisted   ."

no indictment.

this doesn't stop you from wanting
to raise the dead.
this doesn't stop you from considering
and reconsidering "the future life"
of someone's child, now in the ground.
from holding our complicated abused and abusive
bodies not worthy of a casual bullet in the head.

this doesn't stop.
and so you take pause.
look past spectacle.

speculate an other world.
one repossessed
from some discarded archive
organized into existence.

Communiqué #4

trouble always strike from behind
don't know no honest fight
and fear that child - that child - that child –

that child -

all body and love.
all Assata and Shango.
all spirit and unmapped alphabet
charging through they veins.

trouble fear that child might show them up
might make *trouble* reckon with itself
reckon how with all the data and resource and theft of land and
body and capital, that not even no rocket-charged Adidas could
stop this whoopin'.

black black
black black
black black
black black
black black
black black
black black
black black
black black
black black
black black
black black
black black
black black
black black
black black
black black
black black
black black
black black
black black
black black
black black
black black
black black black black black black black black black black black black black black black black or perhaps this is just my way of saying i don't care to be legible.
black black
black black
black black
black black
black black
black black
black black
black black
black black
black black
black black
black black
black black
black black
black black
black black
black black
black black
black black
black black
black black
black black
black black
black black
black black
black black
black black
black black
black black
black black
black black

1. ~~black~~
2. is
3. a
4. destination
5. N
6. perpetual
7. exile.

Communiqué #5

it didn't take long with child *MOOOOOOOOVVVING*

      across Freemont and Emerson,
      across West Broadway and Vincent
      across Girard and Russell

sprinklin' that Mississippi along the way,
freaking that ground like Robert Johnson's hands did the guitar,
sending out a sort of dispatch - some kind of NEW JIVE BOOGIE -
a magic in them words about

the strength of child's feet,
the length of they stride and the intensity of the whoopin'
they bout to wrest up from that ground.
the flies they bout to leave swimming in *trouble's* milk.

- nah it didn't take long for *trouble* to catch wind.

hands wringing,
blood boiling
so hot they was beside theyself.

and sometimes hot blood make for untempered heads.
get one thinking that they badder than they ought to think.
and so *trouble* emerge from an unkempt place -

you know -

| rən |

like high voltage. cloud on your back. see
Shango. faster now. past history - herstory. see
the whole thing play out from a high place. insert
Tubman, Sojourner, Assata. faster now. feet meet
earth in repetition, union - insert bre'r rabbit.
diggin'. roots. as in Baker, Lorde, Davis, Semenya.
outrun gender. faster now. through an escape
route. faster now. mississippi under your feet. break.
free. faster now. become lighting. strike twice

Communiqué #6

that place that know no good.
that geography of bones.
that precint full of lying tongues, and noxious smell,
and boundless animus.

yeah you know that place -
trouble get up from there -
from that place -
and make they way to the corner goooooooood and slooooooooow.

child know *trouble* coming, heard it by now from they kin,
themseleves a constellation of beautiful **black** productions.
yeah child know, and waiting, waiting for *trouble*.

***

a murder of crows *or* **the scene of the crime**

researchers conducted a study finding
that crows remember   well.
that they see their fellow fallen sister
and brother crows and remember the stalking bodies
that go near
identify those looming with danger.
crows will scold and dive at
those who they find holding the remains of their intimates.

though it has always been this way
before the research.
before a dive or chastising
cry became legible.

and somewhere there is a murder
of crows.
a common urban variety
black and concentrated.
watching the remains.
remembering.

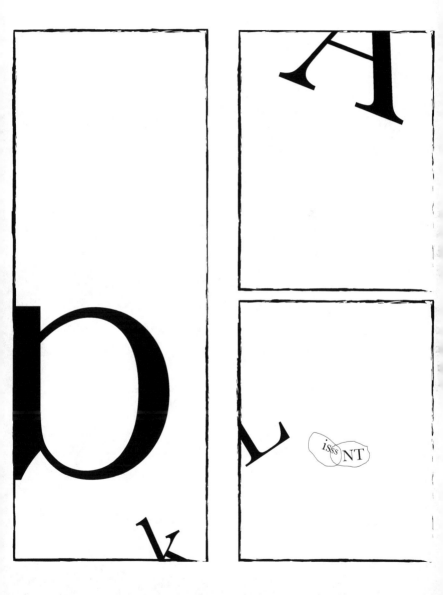

Communiqué #7

that night *trouble* would race the child,

child's kin all up and down Lowry Avenue watching,
no cars,
no observation of street lights,
not even any shoes on child's feet
just a rugged determination to break the sound barrier.

child and *trouble* place they feet on the line
standing between them two pillars on Lowry Ave
faces steely towards north 2nd
where the race would end.

they agree to begin
at the siren
that siren that goes off at 9pm like clockwork
to some fire continuing to erupt.

i don't remember...

you leave one summer. do you remember? that new space,
the dark matter of your body? you left, not many miles,
you moved a bit further north & then to university, do you
remember? that new space, the dark matter of your body?
not thinking of return yet you return do you remember
can you remember a time when you did not feel alien, in-
between borders, fabricated...something was robbed but you
weren't there, do you remember? can you remember the
theft? the compulsory leaving & returning & leaving again.
you leave one summer.   you   ? that new   ,
the dark matter   ? you   , not many miles,
you moved   north & then   , do you
remember?   your body? not
thinking of return   you   do you   can you
                  not feel alien, in-between
borders, fabricated...something   robbed   you
      do you remember?   the theft?
            leaving &   leaving again. you
leave   do you   ? that   space,
            your body? you left,
            further   do you
remember? that   space,   dark matter   ? not
            return yet   return
                  you   feel alien, in between

            leaving & returning
                        that   dark
            body?   left,
                        do you remember?

71

Communiqué #8

you ever wonder if feet hold memory?
if there is somehow a cognizance in bones and muscle
joints and soft tissue carrying child like Harriet's did before
between mason dixie and North Star?

seeing child along Lowry and James,
Lowry and Girard, Lowry and Freemont,
you need not wonder.
child's body had its own vernacular
saying something
always saying.

trouble paddy wagonning as
child re members
re members
re members

cast they body into a story
into a bio myth
like the one they mama told them

of how Tubman managed to fashion her body
into cast metal

how she stripped her skin down to a lead slug and slung herself
from a trusted pistol

time seems trivial when thinking of the aerials of that bullet...
seen now somersaulting past more than mason dixie
seen now maneuvering through the iron ribbed steal
of cages holding those who did not outrun *trouble* --
seen now coaching the memory of feet tired and weary
of running

full turn—

imagine child running

running toward fear at the pace of Madhubuti because the home
we chart is a sky of our own making

and the present has always been a dangerous place
for children who dare to run faster than *trouble*.

do not turn away Sandra
do not turn away Renisha
do not turn away Aiyana
do not turn away child

for when we draw our bodies closer to your feet
we re member also.

run.

**Astro Colony *or* an Obscure Rock in the Milkyway
will Gentrify also: the scene of the crime**

low-capital Blacks - all that detritus and unrest - will be
shipped to outer-space, to the most undesirable
parcel in a single faintly-explored galaxy of the
multiverse. they will be sent, no doubt for their own good,
to this unfamiliar place in the astros. a place decaying but of
unique architectural quality. they, the low-capital Blacks,
will be sent there. way, way, out there. and they will make
lemonade, and chittlings, and will usher some new sound to
shake that little bit of rock until that too becomes a site of
forced removal.

yup...

Notes or an exercise in **Black Annotation** & **Black Redaction**

black bodies *or* the scene of the crime

1. It is quite possible that few things on this earth run slower than the route 19 bus.

2. The black body is "territorialized." Katherine McKittrick writes, "The history of the black diaspora converges with bodily schemas and racial codes. Most obviously, the geographies of transatlantic slavery were geographies of black dispossession and white supremacy, which assumed racial inferiority and justified enslavement. Geographies such as the slave ship, the slave auction block, slave coffles, and the plantation, are just some of the sites of spatialized domination under bodage. In particular, the ties between ownership and blackness rendered the black body a commodity, a site of embodied property, through ideological and economic exchanges... Geographically in the most crude sense, the body is territorialized— it is publicly and financially claimed, owned, and controlled by an outsider." *Demonic Grounds: Black Women And The Cartographies Of Struggle* (Minneapolis: University Of Minnesota Press, 2006), 44. Print.

3. *Stage / as in, the popular theater / of your body.* Your body. Territorialized. A site of performance. Violence? All that terror, and that is terrible, need not be shocking. See Saidiya Hartman. "I have chosen to look elsewhere and consider those scenes in which terror can hardly be discerned—slaves dancing in the quarters, the outrageous darky antics of the minstrel stage, the constitution of humanity in slave law, and the fashioning of the self-possessed individual. By defamiliarizing the familiar, I hope to illuminate the terror of the mundane and quotidian rather than exploit the shocking spectacle." *Scenes Of Subjection: Terror, Slavery, And Self-Making In Nineteenth Century America* (New York: Oxford, 1997), 4. Print.

4.   Elsewhere. See Jayne Cortez. See Robin Kelley. See Baldwin. Try to calculate the price of the ticket.

north minneapolis circa 1492

1.   In the beginning was the northside, and it was a good and layered thing, re: repetition, re: fragments, re: collage as practice in writing and reading. See Romare Bearden. See James Braxton Peterson, *The Hip Hop Underground And African American Culture* (New York: Palgrave, 2014). Print. re: sampling. See *Invisible Man* re: in the beginning...there was blackness. north minneapolis

2.   robbery: the action of robbing a **person** or place: *he was involved in an armed robbery.* Person. Perhaps it is more than a gun to one's temple: *hands in the air! this is a stick up, mutha fucka!* More like our basic assumptions around robbery conceal the biggest heists of the modern world, that modernity itself required such theft. See Baldwin re: *I suspect these stories are designed to reassure us that no crime was committed.* See Ngugi Wa Thiongo, *Something Torn and New.* See that new shit on the corner of your block that *you* can no longer afford, and then, STICK EM UP! robbery: the action of robbing a person or a **place** re: *north minneapolis looks alot like the scene of a robbery circa 1492.* And the land was speculated on in the antebellum south by way of black bodies re: slave labor or cash (crops) rules everything around me! See Enter The Wu-Tang (36 Chambers), See also *The Half Has Never Been Told.* And the land was speculated on in the north by way of black bodies re: negative space, or what exists around the subject image, pronouncing it re: whiteness. robbery: the action of robbing a person or a place. What the fuck is left in your purse?

Do. Not. Enter.

1.   Webster, Chaun. *Do. Not. Enter.* 2016.
2.   How might we go about mapping what is not there, what is missing, and enter the vactated space?

Quantum FEET

1. because restricted movement. because imagined shifting boundaries imposing a kind of nomadic statelessness. & yet more so because fugitivity. because *the child runs faster than trouble*. because maroonage was/is a daily political practice of return and return is some complicated shit (see Hartman, see Butler) that refuses to follow a straight line.

Communiqué de Whoopin': *or the child runs faster than trouble*

1. got Assata feet / got Tubman in they soles / run like Usain they do.
2. Niggas been runnin'. Both to, and from.
3. Neil Roberts writes, "Marronage (marronnage, maroonage, maronage) conventionally refers to a group of persons isolating themselves from a surrounding society in order to reate a fully autonomous community, and for centuries it has been integral to interpreting the idea of freedom in Haiti as well as other Caribbean islands and Latin American countries including the Dominican Republic, Jamaica, Suriname, Venezuela, Brazil, Cuba, Colombia, and Mexico." *Freedom As Marronage* (Chicago: University of Chicago Press, 2015), 4. Print.
4. "time would pass, old empires would fall and new ones take their place, the relations of classes had to change, before I discovered that it is not quality of goods and utility which matter, but movement; not where you are or what you have, but where you have come from, where you are going and the rate at which you are getting there." James, C.L.R. *Beyond a Boundary* (Durham: Duke University Press, 2013), 113. Print.
5. See Alexis De Veaux. *Yabo*, "there are other heres" (11). Give thanks.
6. General Sylvanus Lowry was the first mayor of St. Cloud Minnesota; they also owned enslaved Africans. Stats for your ass.
7. This whole scene takes place on Lowry Avenue, not named after the aforementioned mark Sylvanus, but yet another white thief (redundant much?) out of Illinois.

8. At Lowry and Penn, there sits one of the many liquor stores in this small geography. Believe me when I say that shit opens at 8am, while the elementary school next store doesn't open until 8:25.

legibility *or* the scene of the crime

1. Question: is illegibility the same as invisibility? If not, if the illegible is din *(din has its own discourse)* then is there some use to illegiblity, read blackness, that disturbs the grid of comprehension? See Glissant, Edouard. *Carribean Discourse: Selected Essays* (Charlottesville: University Press of Virginia, 1999), 123. Print. See Christina Sharpe re: Black Redaction, Black Annotation, and our, *refusals ot accede to optics*. *In the Wake: On Blackness and Being* (Durham: Duke University Press, 2016), 115. Print. Now you see me... now you don't.

2. Everything hinges on this. The repetition. The feedback. A proposed means of getting at Sharpe's redaction and annotation, *"toward seeing and reading otherwise; toward reading and seeing something in excess of what is caught in the frame; toward seeing something beyond a visuality that is* (117). I cannot go anywhere, but: the crime. I cannot go anywhere, but: black life in excess of the crime.

"i don't want no fucking country"

1. In the beginning was the northside, and it was good, and we didn't want no fucking country neither. See Brand, Dionne. *Land to Light On* (Toronto: McClelland & Stewart, 1997), 48. Print.

black bodies en fugue

1. The entirety of this piece is the superimposition re: sampling of a portion of an essay by Bench Ansfield entitled, "Still Submerged: The Uninhabitability of Urban Redevelopment" which can be found in the anthology *Sylvia Wynter: On Being Human As Praxis* edited by Katherine McKittrick, (128). Read that.

2. McKittrick notes the common sense of black displacement saying, "the production of black spaces in the diaspora is tied to locations

that were and are explicitly produced in conjunction with race, racism, captivity and economic profit. Traditional geographies did, and arguably still do, *require* black displacement, black placelessness, black labor, and a black population that submissively stays 'in plac.'" *Demonic Grounds: Black Women And The Cartographies Of Struggle* (Minneapolis: University of Minnesota Press, 2006), 9. Print.

3.   fugue: a contrapunal composition in which a short melody or phrase (the subject) is introduced by one part successively taken up by others and developed into interweaving parts re: excess. "The fugue has, however, another darker meaning, referring to a state of amnesia in which the individual, his or her subjectivity having been destroyed, becomes alienated from him - or herself. It is a state that can be as brief as a few hours or as lengthy as several years. In its erasure and forgetting of the be-ing and humanity of the Africans on board the *Zong*, the legal text of *Gregson v. Gilbert* becomes a representation of the fugal state of amnesia, serving as a mechanism for erasure and alienation. Further, in my fragmenting of the text and re-writing it through *Zong!*, or rather over it, thereby essentially erasing it, the orignal text becomes a fugal plimpsest through which *Zong!* is allowed to heal the original text of its fugal amnesia." See M. NourbeSe Phillip. *Zong!* (Middletown: Wesleyan University Press, 2008), 204. Print.

4.   What of the precarity of blackness, extended, *extra*territorial? What of the tendency to naturalize the conditions of concentration? *A geography is designed. A geography is illegible.* re: legibility *or* the scene of the crime. How do we document place and the black body, the black body, the black body—superimposed—recognizing the role of coloniality in its movement without re-inscribing it as only acted upon?

Theft *or* the scene of the crime

1.   Alternative titles being: *On stolen land hardly a day goes by where I am not accused of stealing, or America's back rent is incalculable but my manager think the register is under cuz of my black hand, or If North Migrating Niggas was considered contraband are they capable of theft? or What happens when black*

things accused of theft, when—everywhere the robbery—cannot find a single fuck to give? re: Baldwin, *i suspect all these stories...*

2. Fundamental contradiction: North Minneapolis, although having depreciated land value, cuz...niggas, is a desirable geography with undesirable bodies, which is to say, niggas.

Communiqué #1

1. See Walker, David. *Appeal To The Coloured Citizens Of The World* (Philadelphia: Penn University Press, 2000). Print.

2. Walker was fucking with trouble too. A Boston free black. Wrote a piece that went something like viral for its time. Niggas read that shit to each other like the good news. Said in no uncertain terms that the almighty was cool if niggas fucked massa up. Made Garrison's ACS supporting ass get his shit together. Scared the hell outta any white folks that heard it whispered. Them white folks put a hit out for Walker, and that free black man would turn up dead, and them same white folks gonna say something like it was tuberculosis. But niggas know better and one day someone gonna write that whole story.

3. Audre Lorde instructed her students to keep a dream journal. Lorde still teaching, and we need do our best to listen.

nah...

1. Nah; short for, *"nah nigga."*

maybe home

1. What happens to essentialist notions of blackness once sturdy ground is shaken? Is it biological? National re: where your ancestors happened to land? Phenotypic? Who can appropriate it (See, *Appropriating Blackness: Performance and the Politics of Authenticity* by E. Patrick Harris)? How do we begin to map belonging in terms of our own making?

2. In so many formulations of black "nationhood" or black

86

collective identity there is an assumed Middle Passage epistemology (see Michele M. Wright, *Physics of Blackness*) that cannot encompass the many strands of this instable signifier, re: *The Autobiography of Leroi Jones*, "Home, which meant coming back to one's self, ones consciousness, coming back to blackness. I ended the introduction to the book: 'By the time you read this, I will be even blacker.' That was true, albeit the grand stance. But I could also have said: 'and confused like a motherfucker.' But, at least, I was literally, Home." (328)

because apparently no one woke up on they john wayne shit to take land. it just happened...

1. How to distance yourself from the naturalizing of the taking: *it just happened.* The theft becomes hard to name, as does the thief: *apparently no one woke up on they John Wayne shit. It just happened.* The taking is everywhere, and everywhere it is obscured.

2. When thinking of settler colonialism, the land becomes metaphor for the body re: the 1492 framework of the North American land and subsequently indigenous peoples' are considered barren, uncivilized, and empty. Gentrification hinges on the same logic and blackness often becomes the shorthand that mediates the understanding of barren, uncivilized, and empty land re: North Minneapolis, in need of revitalization. See *Sylvia Wynter: On Being Human As Praxis* Edited by Katherine McKittrick. See *Demonic Grounds: Black Women And The Cartographies Of Struggle* by Katherine McKittrick.

3. This connection between displacement, settler colonialism and black bodies is spoken to also in Tiffany King's article, *One Strike Evictions, State Space, and the Production of Abject Black Female Bodies,* where King speaking to the technology of the One Strike Eviction says, "Tracing US colonialism and the institution of slavery in Tampa reveals a history of dual processes of native extermination and black enslavement in this region in Florida. US colonialism and slavery are/were dual processes of capial accumulation that determined land tenure and land use practices in Tampa. Black struggle in the

swamplands of Florida took on an explicitly anti-colonial politic due to the expansion of slavery through US colonialism in Florida in the 19th century. The legacy of resistance to US colonialism, black spatial domination and explotiation continues today in the struggle Burton and other blacks (possibly descendants of 'Black Seminoles') wage against the One Strike law and gentrification in Tampa...Naming policies like One Strike as colonial technologies of eviction allows for the introduction of some significant analytical interventions. For one, it enables us to historicize the U.S. as a settler-colonial state that continually accumulates capital through projects of native genocide and black containment and exploitation."

4. Latorious, Latoria, and Latorianna, were consumed by fire that erupted from a stove left on to heat a home on Penn Avenue N. re: *no more no   more   no more*. Say their names and restore their life. What of the disposability of the black wageless poor? What of the technologies of their disposability, substandard housing, not inconsequential among them? Fire in North Minneapolis has contributed to the spatial movement of low income residents, many of whom are black, in ways that has me asking: can a city be charged with arson?

this is not a black *Atlantic*

1. See Gilroy, Paul. *The Black Atlantic: Modernity and Double-Consciousness* (Boston: Harvard University Press, 1993). Print. Been tryin to reckon with Genesis re: beginnnings, as they relate to notions of morpheus' *desert of the real*. Been trying to peel back, get up under the signifier, cuz, "even to think in terms of falsification is to fall victim to a ploy, to authenticity's traps. And therein lies race's social power— it's ability to evade the most careful and rigorous of social scientific analyses. The ethnographic goal, then, is not to look for something redemptive about race (an intellectual wild goose chase if ever there was one), **but rather to find the pockets of qualitative possibility that mystify the mathematical equations people use for figuring self and other in contemporary societies overdetermined by race**—an overdetermination that begs for

88

some recognition of the symbolic remainders that exceed naively rationalist and realist responses." John L. Jackson Jr., *Real Black: Adventures In Racial Sincerity* (58, 59). So if you asking what it is and catch an *Out & Gone* expression re: Baraka, know this: the aim been to mystify.

2. In 1935 UMN graduate student Calvin Schmidt was federally funded to publish a series of maps. These were a part of a larger study titled, *Social Saga of Two Cities*. In it Schmidt identifies a portion of North Minneapolis as the "Negro Slum", even though in 1930, Hennepin County—a much more significant geography that North Minneapolis lay within—had its first census showing the "Negro" population to be less than 1%. Moral: Schmidt was fabricating Negroes, or at the very least overdetermining our social, and thereby, geographic location.For more on *fabricated presence*, See Toni Morrison's, *Playing in the Dark: Whiteness and the Literary Imagination*, which examines this fabrication in Western canonical literary texts.

gentry

1. Gentry, *That frown should have told you the city was not the town. They were in the future, like Dis, Like Capital, Like Hades when it was Havies. It's heavy. It's still Havies...You created Hollywood because you didn't want to talk. You made the woman feline so you could teach philosophy while you was asleep. So you created youself as the answer to what you souldn't have asked.* See Amiri Barka, *"What Is Undug Will Be", Tales Of The Out & The Gone* (157)

Communiqué #2

1. Sandra Bland lived and was disappeared within a cell in Waller County Texas July 13, 2015. Say her name, and restore her life.
2. Or maybe: which is to say trouble that as distinct as Plymouth Avenue, Waller County and a doorstep in Dearborn Heights Michigan are from each other re: scenes of the crime, they are the handiwork of trouble.

this is not a ~~black.~~ and it is.

1. less statement, more query on the limits of representation re: black is...and it ain't, see Ellison, see Douglas Kearney, see Benston, see Rhodes-Pitts. look over the Atlantic, past middle passage epistomologies and see you many varied self black re: *Physics of Blackness.* like what is the matter of this thing? and if performative, than so little stability in this thing: so why so rigid my nigga?

talking commodities *or* the scene of the crime

1. Read from Marx that commodities do not engage in the normative functions of subjects. Commodities do not speak.
2. What are niggas but this country's fundamental contradiction? bought and sold american blacks, yet talking. *Din is discourse.* Glissant. More on that later.
3. Fred Moten writes, "The history of blackness is testament to the fact that objects can and do resist." *In The Break: The Aesthetics Of The Black Radical Tradition* (Minneapolis: University of Minnesota Press, 2003), 1. Print.

N's in molecular type

1. Molecular typography, or, the study of letters through their physical and chemical underpinnings. See, *Breaking Type: The Story Of Molecular Typography.* See, *Understanding Molecular Typography.*
2. If letters are formed from interchangeable parts, what parts form the N (shorthand for nigga)?
3. "I think if one examines the myths chich have proliferated in this country concerning the negro one discovers that beneath these myths is a kind of sleeping terror of some condition which we refuse to imagi N e." See Baldwin, James. "Birmingham and Beyond: The Negro's Push for Equality." *Time* May 1963. *content. time.com* Web. 28 Aug. 2017.
4. Cedric Robinson writes, "The 'Negro,' that is the color black was both a negation of Africa and **a unity of opposition to white.**

The construct of Negro, unlike the terms 'African,' 'Moor,' or 'Ethiope,' suggested no situatedness in time, that is history, or space, that is ethno- or politico-geography. The Negro had no civilization, no cultures no religions, no history, no place, and finally no humanity that might command consideration." *Black Marxism: The Making of the Black Radical Tradition* (Chapel Hill: University of North Carolina Press, 2000), 81. Print.

5. White subjectivity ain't shit without a "Negro."
6. For every "Southwest" there is a "Northside." See Smith, Neil. *Development: Nature, Capital ,and the Production of Space* (Athens: University of Georgia Press, 3rd edition, 2008). Print.

forbidDIN

1. "Noise is essential to speech. Din is discourse. This must be understood." See Edouard Glissant, *Caribbean Discourse: Selected Essays*, (123).
2. Blackness and black geographies—see Katherine McKittrick and Clyde Woods—though often illegible and made imperceptible by a variety of technologies, are not invisible. We here.
3. In the noise the clamor, the illogic, the blackness, is a vernacular apart. Subversive. forbiDIN. *noise is essential to speech, noise is essential to speech, noise is essential to speech, noise is essential to speech, noise is essential to speech, noise is essential to speech, noise is essential to speech, noise is essential to speech, noise is essential to speech, noise is essential to speech, noise is essential to speech, noise is essential*

Communiqué #3

1. The Mississippi brings life, has its birth in Northern Minnesota, connects the state of Minnesota to the south far too often overdetermined as the scene of the crime. But, *"NIGGAS KNOW BETTER / THAN ANYBODY EVEN THIS COUNTRY'S LOVE SMELLS OF GUNPOWDER"* re: Douglas Kearney, Quantum Spit. Which is to say, everywhere the crime. Which is to say everywhere black life, in excess of the crime.
2. Lorde, Davis, Smith, Wells-Barnett and so many other texts are sacred, are portals. Praise the Lorde.

this is not a black: an abstraction of a nonessential thing

1. Michelle M. Wright writes that, "to understand Blackness as a construct without explaining what it is—only what it is not—generates old and new paradoxes in our arguments. The largest problem is that of unequal representation of Black collectives in discourses of Blackness generally: despite our best efforts, some groups enjoy being understood as Black, whereas others have to struggle and clamor for recognition. The 'problem' is hardly limited to our most heavily burdensome to scholars who work in Black American history and culture—it is, I would argue, endemic to any and all discourses on Blackness that reject a biological origin for race and yet offer little else in its place." See Wright, Michelle M. *Physics Of Blackness: Beyond The Middle Passage Epistemology* (Minneapolis: University of Minnesota Press, 2015), 3. Print.

2. What it is though?

GeNtry!fication: a 21st century disappearing act

1. disappearance *noun* an instance or fact of someone or something ceasing to be visible. What happens when we read the phenomenon of gentrification through the magic trick, the sleight of hand? Does this visibility, this *ceasing to be visible*, register more as a kind of missing in plain sight than a ceasing to be visible? Could removal be a kind of sleight of hand? But then something necessarily remains, even if only faintly.

2. Kevin Young writes in his book, *The Grey Album: On The Blackness Of Blackness*, about the idea of the shadow book, or, "a book that we don't have, but know of, a book that may haunt the very book that we have in our hands." (11) And geography is a text. It may be read. And geography is not just material, but imagined, remembered. So whose book are we left with when the once, undesirable space, black geography, outside of value (see Lindon Barrett) is now speculated on and pioneered to the extent of *ain't nothing left...but the shadow.*

i remember

1. M. Jaqui Alexander, considering the impact of the anthology, *This Bridge Called My Back*, asks, "Can we intentionally remember, all the time, as a way of never forgetting, all of us, building an archeology of living memory, which has less to do with living the past, invoking a past or excising it, and more to do with our relationship to Time and its purpose? There is a difference between remembering when— the nostalgic yearning for some return—and a living memory that enables us to remember what was contained in Bridge and what could not be contained within it or by it. What did it make possible? What else did we need? All are part of this living memory, of moments, of imaginings, which have never ended. And they will never end so long as we continue to dare yearning for each other. There is a writing exercise that Natalie Goldberg, author of *Thunder and Lightning*, has popularized. For ten minutes, or some designated time, the exercise participant is asked to write uninterruptedly, beginning with 'I remember,' so long as to bring to the present all things remembered. The exercise is then reversed with its supposed opposite: 'I don't remember.' As one participant negotiated the underbelly of her recollections, she observed, 'It scares me that I remember what I don't remember.'" *Pedagogies of Crossing: Meditations On Feminism, Sexual Politics, Memory, And The Sacred* (Durham: Duke University Press, 2005), 278. Print.

bodies out of place

1. On November 15th, 2015 Jamar Clark was extra judicially killed by members of the Minneapolis Police Department. Say his name, and restore his life.
2. McKittrick again is useful here, telling us that, "Traditional geographies did, and arguably still do, *require* black displacement, black placelessness, black labor, and a black population that submissively stays 'in place.' *Demonic Grounds: Black Women And The Cartographies Of Struggle* (Minneapolis: University of Minnesota Press, 2006), 9. Print.

3. Simone Brown writes, "the *Book of Negroes* is an early imprint of how the body comes to be understood as a means of identification and tracking by the state...the *Book of Negroes* became the first large-scale public record of black presence in North America. This handwritten and leather-bound British military ledger lists three thousand black passengers who left New York in 1783...the making of the *Book of Negroes* offers a historicizing of the ways in which tracking, accounting, and identification of the racial body, and in particular the black body and black social life, form an important, but often absented, part of the genealogy of the passport." *Dark Matters: On The Surveillance Of Blackness* (Durham: Duke University Press, 2015), 70. Print. Put this in the context of a shot-spotter, of civilian and police recordings of murder, and facial recognition software. Then smile wide, you on camera.

4. See June Jordan, "Nobody Mean More to Me Than You and the Future Life of Willie Jordan" *Some of Us Did Not Die: New and Selected Essays of June Jordan* (New York: Basic/Civitas Books, 2003), 157-173

5. "*holding our complicated abused and abusive / bodies not worthy of a casual bullet in the head.*" At times I am concerned that we who are concerned about the violence the state uses on black bodies are in search of the "perfect black victim." That there is a real, often unstated, fear of how much slimmer the already slim chances for justice will mean if the victim of state violence had a weapon, or talked back or used an illegal substance beforehand or was involved in intimate partner violence. This is not to say we do not need to reckon with the choices of these individuals, only that those choices do not warrant the violence the state often brings disproportionately on them. It may be time to re-examine commitments to the notion of innocence, which I see being used more often than not to create a hierarchy distinguishing (howevery shakily) some from the *common sense* of the disposability of the black *wageless poor*. See Melamed, Jodi. *Represent And Destroy: Rationalizing Violence In The New Racial Capitalism* (Minneapolis: University Of Minnesota, 2011), 120. Print.

6. Joy James and João Costa Vargas ask, "What happens when instead of becoming enraged and shocked every time a Black person is killed in the United States, we recognize Black death as

a predictable and constitutive aspect of this democracy? What will happen then if instead of demanding justice we recognize (or at least consider) that the very notion of justice...produces and requires Black exclusion and death as normative." James, Joy, and João Costa Vargas. "Refusing Blackness-as-Victimization: Trayvon Martin and the Black Cyborgs." In *Pursuing Trayvon: Historical Contexts and Contemporary Manifestations of Racial Dynamics*, edited by George Yancy and Janine Jones (Latham: Lexington Books, 2012), 193-205.

darkMATTER *or* detour

1. Neil Smith writes, "*Détour* is the desire to acquire freedom in a place or medium other than your transplanted homeland. Glissant conceives of *détour* to be both a trickster strategy and camouflage." *Freedom As Marronage* (Chicago: University of Chicago Press, 2015), 157. Print.

2. **"Kameelah Rasheed:** We are at a point in history when visibility and inclusion are often conflated with radical change. If I hire a black person to be a screenwriter on my show, then radical change has occurred; if a person from a marginalized community who doesn't traditionally get to be in the spotlight gets their fifteen minutes then, woah!, radical change has occurred. I'm really interested in interrogating visibility as a concession, as a premature celebration, because visibility in and of itself without the rigor of analyzing why certain people were invisible to begin with is limited. It is much more productive to think about how individuals can become not the first and only but the first of many. I'm really focused on distinguishing between the optics of diversity and the actual structural impact of diversity. Everyone wants to hire a black person at their job, everyone wants to have a party around diversity, but are they really willing to do the work and make the sacrifices to get their organization (or our nation) to make structural change? That doesn't come from cherry-picking people who will be hoisted up as markers of inclusion. At times we become fascinated or almost obsessed with symbols and with the optics of things without unpacking the impact that those symbols and those optics have. There is a lot of focus on

always showing your hand, and always telling people what you are doing—always asking for hyper-visibility as a radical move. But a lot of the radical work done in movements prior to our generation was not necessarily done through hyper-visibility. People covertly published things, and covertly educated people, and covertly got training. So I'm interested in how we can think about, not so much hiding, but strategic opaqueness—refusing to be legible." Rasheed, Kameelah. Interview by Imani Roach. "Kameelah Rasheed: Who Will Survive in America" *Guernica*, 6 Mar. 2017, https://www.guernicamag.com/kameelah-rasheed-who-will-survive-in-america/?platform=hootsuite. And if it isn't abundantly clear by now, I'm with Kameelah.

3. See Simone Brown, "Prototypical whiteness...is the cultural logic that informs much of biometric information technology. It sees whiteness, or lightness, as privileged in enrollment, measurement, and recognition processes, and...prototypical whiteness is reliant upon dark matter for its own meaning. Dark matter being those bodies and body parts that trouble some biometric technology, like dark irises or cameras that 'can't see black people' or that ask some Asian users, 'Did someone blink?' When particular surveillance technologies, in their development and design, leave out some subjects and communities for optimum usage, this leaves open the possibility of reproducing existing inequalities. This point is somewhat upheld in a 2010 U.S. National Research Council report on biometrics which argued that it is 'incumbent upon those who conceive, design and deploy biometric systems to consider the cultural, social and legal contexts of these systems. Not attending to these consdierations and failing to consider their social impacts diminishes their efficacy and can bring serious unintended consequences, like further marginalization, and in some cases the disenfranchisement, of people who because of industry-determined standard algorithms encounter difficulty in using this technology. **When dark matter troubles algorithms in this way, it amounts to a refusal of the idea of neutrality when it comes to certain technologies. But if algorithms can be troubled, this might not necessarily be a bad thing. In other words, could there be some potential in going**

about unknown or unremarkable, and perhaps unbothered
, where CCTV, camera-enabled devices, facial recognition,
and other computer technologies are in use?" *Dark Matters: On
The Surveillance Of Blackness* (Durham: Duke University Press, 2015),
162, 163. Print. Emphasis mine.

blackness is a constant act of flight

1. See, runaway notice, see the pseudo science of draeptomania, see Virgina Hamilton *The People Could Fly* and know that as long as there have been restrictions on black movement, there have been the transgressions to those restrictions.
2. "Marronage is a multidimensional, constant act of flight." Smith, Neil. *Freedom As Marronage* (Chicago: University of Chicago Press, 2015), 9. Print.
3. Blackness is marronage.

foot notes

1. rən, as shorthand for fugitivity. rən as both kinesthetic and discursive methodology. rən, as a means to roots & escape routes. a form of sampling.
2. The rən, or the track, in this case graphic unit/sign can have a rhizomatic quality. Roots/routes have no time, is "always in the middle between things." See Braxton Peterson, James. *The Hip-Hop Underground And African American Culture* (New York: Palgrave Macmillian, 2014), 2. Print. See Deleuze. Rən tell that.
3. When rən-ing read the ground. read the temperature the soil, feet fresh upon it. See Grant, Richard. "Deep in the Swamps, Archaeologists Are Finding How Fugitive Slaves Kept Their Freedom." Smithsonian Magazine, Sept. 2016, http://www.smithsonianmag.com/history/deep-swamps-archaeologists-fugitive-slaves-kept-freedom-180960122/?no-ist

a murder of crows *or* the scene of the crime

1. "Crows and humans share the ability to recognize faces and associate them with negative, as well as positive, fellings. The way the brain activates during that process is something the two species also appear to share, according to new research being published this week. The regions of the crow brain that work together are not unlike those that work together in mammals, including humans." Hines, Sandra. "Crows react to threats in human-like way." University of Washington News, Sept. 2012, http://www.washington.edu/news/2012/09/10/crows-react-to-threats-in-human-like-way/

this is not a black: a note on instability.

1. See "Is, Ain't" Kearney, Douglas. *Skin Mag* (New York: Deadly Chaps, 2011), 10. Print.

DARKmatter *or* retour

1. Neil Smith writes, "*Retour* is the yearning to return to a single origin and fixed state of being. Glissant argues that individuals or groups who have been transplanted by force from one location to another develop an obsession with finding strategies to recreate lost primordial customs and ways of life and to return to an original ancestral locale...*Retour*, however, becomes impossible the longer a population has insufficient knowledge of its past. Prolonged distance from an ancestral land dissipates the insidious effects of the desire to imitate the unattainable." *Freedom As Marronage* (Chicago: University of Chicago Press, 2015), 157. Print.

Communiqué #8

1. See Madhabuti, Haki. *Run Toward Fear: New Poems and a Poet's Handbook* (Chicago: Third World Press, 2004). Print.

Astro Colony or an Obscure Rock in the Milkyway will Gentrify also: the scene of the crime

1. "Baby Suggs grew tired, went to bed and stayed there until her big old heart quit. Except for an occasional quest for color she said practically nothing—until the afternoon of the last day of her life when she got out of her bed, skipped slowly to the door of the keeping room and announced to Sethe and Denver the lesson she had learned from her sixty years a slave and ten years free: that there was no bad luck in the world but white-people. 'They don't know when to stop,' she said." Morrison, Toni. *Beloved* (New York, Vintage; Reprint Edition, 2004). Print.

2. "*until that too becomes a site of forced removal.*" Cuz, Capital, like white folks/ness, "*don't know when to stop*" either.

3. The, "*until that too becomes a site of forced removal*" is less nihilism than trying to examine the recurrent text of forced removal and limitations of activist interventions to this absenting of bodies and memory. We still gon' *shake that little bit of rock* though. We still gon need to do more.

4. If this is the history, the past, the question becomes, "What is the future? The future has been around so long it is now the past. Afro-Surrealists expose this form a 'future-past' called RIGHT NOW." Scott Miller, D. *AFROSURREAL MANIFESTO: Black is the new black* (Chicago: Epicenter, 2012). Print.

gawn!

1. Kevin Young writes, "We are the ones on the plantation speaking and singing to each other in *code*, to let others know our intent—such ar and artfulness precede what sets us free, and more often than not, are the code by which that freedom is achieved. If we cannot first imagine freedom, we cannot actually achieve it. Freedom, like fiction and all art, is a process in which the dream of freedom is only the first part. Rather than stay in their place, the slaves imagined a new one. Remapping was for the slave a necessary form of survival— reconfiguring the American landscape as Egypt or Canaan in

order to shore up (and keep secret) their search for freedom. **At times allegorical, always coded, such remappings—a kind of storying—provided a set of radical metaphors for the slaves exile."** *The Grey Album: On The Blackness of Blackness* (Minneapolis: Graywolf Press, 2012), 21. Print. Emphasis mine.

2. "JB: One of the dangers of being a Black American is being schizophrenic, and I mean 'schizophrenic' in the most literal sense. To be a Black American is in some ways to be born with the desire to be white. It's a part of the price you pay for being born here, and it affects every Black person. We can go back to Vietnam, we can go back to Korea. We can go back for that matter to the First World War. We can go back to W.E.B. Du Bois – an honorable and beautiful man – who campaigned to persuade Black people to fight in the First World War, saying that if we fight in this war to save this country, our right to citizenship can never, never again be questioned – and who can blame him? He really meant it, and if I'd been there at that moment I would have said so too perhaps. Du Bois believed in the American dream. So did Martin. So did Malcolm. So do I. So do you. That's why we're sitting here. AL: I don't, honey. I'm sorry, I just can't let that go past. Deep, deep, deep down **I know that dream was never mine.** And I wept and I cried and I fought and I stormed, but I just knew it. **I was Black. I was female. And I was out – out –** by any construct wherever the power lay. So if I had to claw myself insane, if I lived I was going to have to do it alone. Nobody was dreaming about me. Nobody was even studying me except as something to wipe out." Baldwin, James Lorde, Audre "Revolutionary Hope: A Conversation Between James Baldwin And Audre Lorde" *ESSENCE*, 1984.

3. I'm interested in how we might read Lorde's out-ness as a sanctuary, as another articulation of Brand's "I don't want no fucking country" as a lack of investment in the slim promises of this nation of theft (everywhere the crime), as another way of being gawn!

4. Gawn, as practice in fugitivity, as marronage. Gawn, like the body absent, not absented, and still haunting. Like the ghost, holy, tongue speaking din, *speaking and singing to each other in code.* **I was out.** And so it be.

Bibliography / Nods / Samples

And Suggested Tea

Alexander, Elizabeth. *The Black Interior: Essays*. Graywolf Press, 2004.

Alexander, M. Jacqui. *Pedagogies of Crossing: Meditations on Feminism, Sexual Politics, Memory, and the Sacred*. Duke University Press, 2005.

Alexander, Will, et al. *Singing in Magnetic Hoofbeat: Essays, Proese Texts, Interviews And A Lecture 1991-2007*. Essays Press, 2012.

Ansfield, Bench. "Still Submerged: The Uninhabitability of Urban Redevelopment" *Sylvia Wynter on Being Human as Praxis*, edited by Katherine McKittrick. Duke University Press, 2012.

Baraka, Imamu Amiri. T*ales of the out & the Gone*. Akashic Books, 2007.

Barrett, Lindon. *Blackness and Value: Seeing Double*. Cambridge University Press, 1999.

Brand, Dionne. *A Map to the Door of No Return: Notes to Belonging*. Vintage Canada, 2002.

Brand, Dionne. *Inventory*. McClelland & Stewart, 2006.

Brand, Dionne. *Land to Light On*. McClelland & Stewart, 1997.

Browne, Simone. *Dark Matters: on the Surveillance of Blackness*. Duke University Press, 2015.

Bryant, Tisa. *Unexplained Presence*. Leon Works, 2007.

Cha, Theresa Hak Kyung. *Dictee*. Univ. of California Press, 2009.

Cho, Grace M. *Haunting the Korean Diaspora: Shame, Secrecy, and the Forgotten War*. University of Minnesota Press, 2008.

Civil, Gabrielle. *Swallow the Fish: a Memoir in Performance Art*. #RE
CURRENT Novel Series, an Imprint of Civil Coping
Mechanisms, 2017.

Crawley, Ashon T. *Blackpentecostal Breath: the Aesthetics of Possibility*.
Fordham University Press, 2017.

Davis, Thadious M. *Southscapes Geographies of Race, Region, and Literature*.
The University of North Carolina Press, 2014.

Diggs, LaTasha N. Nevada. *Twerk*. Belladonna, 2013.

Ferguson, Roderick A. *Aberrations in Black: toward a Queer of Color
Critique*. University of Minnesota Press, 2004.

Glissant, Edouard. *Caribbean Discourse: Selected Essays*. University Press
of Virginia, 1999.

Gooden, Mario. *Dark Space: Architecture, Representation, Black Identity*.
Columbia Books on Architecture and the City, 2016.

Gumbs, Alexis Pauline. *Spill: Scenes of Black Feminist Fugitivity*. Duke
University Press, 2016.

Harney, Stefano, and Fred Moten. *The Undercommons: Fugitive Planning
and Black Study*. Minor Compositions, 2013.

Hartman, Saidiya. *Lose Your Mother: a Journey along the Atlantic Slave
Route*. Farrar, Straus & Giroux, 2008.

Hartman, Saidiya. *Scenes of Subjection: Terror, Slavery, and Self-Making in
Nineteenth-Century America*. Oxford Univ. Press, 2010.

hooks, bell. *Black Looks: Race and Representation*. Routledge, 2015.

Jackson, John L. *Real Black: Adventures in Racial Sincerity*. University of
Chicago Press, 2005.

James, Joy, and João Costa Vargas. "Refusing Blackness-as-
Victimization: Trayvon Martin and the Black Cyborgs." *Pursuing
Trayvon: Historical Contexts and Contemporary Manifestations of Racial
Dynamics*, edited by George Yancy and Janine Jones. Latham:
Lexington Books, 2012.

Jordan, June. *Some of Us Did Not Die: New and Selected Essays*. Basic/
  Civitas Books, 2003.

Kapil, Bhanu. *Schizophrene*. Nightboat Books, 2011.

Kearney, Douglas. *The Black Automaton*. Fence Books, 2012.

Kearney, Douglas. *Buck Studies*. Fence Magazine, Incorporated, 2016.

Kearney, Douglas. *Mess And Mess And*. Noemi Press, 2015.

Kearney, Douglas. *Quantum Spit: a Poem*. Corollary Press, 2010.

Kearney, Douglas. *Skin Mag*. New York: Deadly Chaps, 2011.

Kinkaid, Jamaica. *A Small Place*. Farrar, Straus and Giroux, 2000.

McKittrick, Katherine, and Clyde Woods. *Black Geographies and the
  Politics of Place*. Between the Lines, 2007.

McKittrick, Katherine. *Demonic Grounds Black Women and the
  Cartographies of Struggle*. Univ. of Minnesota Press, 2006.

Melamed, Jodi. *Represent and Destroy: Rationalizing Violence in the New
  Racial Capitalism*. Univ. of Minnesota Press, 2011.

Miller, D. Scot. *Afrosurreal Manifesto: Black Is the New Black: a 21st Century
  Manifesto*. Epicenter, 2012.

Miles, Tiya. *Ties That Bind: the Story of an Afro-Cherokee Family in Slavery
  and Freedom*. University of California Press, 2015.

Morrison, Toni. *Beloved*. Vintage, 2016.

Morrison, Toni. *Playing in the Dark: Whiteness and the Literary Imagination*.
  Vintage Books, a Division of Random House, Inc, 2015.

Moten, Fred. *In the Break: the Aesthetics of Black Radical Tradition*.
  University of Minnesota Press, 2003.

Peterson, J. *Hip-Hop Underground and African American Culture: Beneath the
  Surface*. Palgrave Macmillan, 2015.

Petti, Alessandro, et al. *Architecture after Revolution*. Sternberg Press,
  2013.

Philip, Marlene Nourbese. *She Tries Her Tongue, Her Silence Softly Breaks*. Wesleyan University Press, 2014.

Philip, Marlene Nourbese. *Zong!* Wesleyan University Press, 2011.

Rhodes-Pitts, Sharifa. *Harlem Is Nowhere: a Journey to the Mecca of Black America*. Back Bay Books/Little, Brown, 2013.

Roberts, Neil. *Freedom as Marronage*. Univ. of Chicago Press, 2015.

Schein, Richard H. *Landscape and Race in the United States*. Routledge, 2006.

Schmid, Calvin F. *Your Minneapolis: an Abstract of Social Saga of Two Cities*. Minneapolis Board of Education, 1938.

Singh, Nikhil Pal. *Black Is a Country: Race and the Unfinished Struggle for Democracy*. Harvard University Press, 2005.

Smith, Neil. *Uneven Development: Nature, Capital, and the Production of Space*. Verso, 2010.

Veaux, Alexis De. *Yabo*. Redbone Press, 2014.

Walker, Alice. *In Search of Our Mothers' Gardens: Womanist Prose*. Harcourt, 2004.

Williamson, Terrion L. *Scandalize My Name: Black Feminist Practice and the Making of Black Social Life*. Fordham University Press, 2017.

Wright, Michelle M. *Physics of Blackness: beyond the Middle Passage Epistemology*. University of Minnesota Press, 2015.

Wynter, Sylvia. *No Humans Involved*. Moor's Head Press, 2016.

Young, Kevin. *The Grey Album: on the Blackness of Blackness*. Graywolf Press, 2012.